Living in the Spirit:

The Lost Secret That Lets Christianity Work

Galen Sharp

ISBN-13: 978-0-9873806-6-1

Living In the Spirit: The Lost Secret That Lets Christianity Work / Galen Sharp

River Of Life Publications

Cover design by Mercedes Piñera

Author Photo by Glenn Cuerden

Printed in the United States of America

This book is dedicated to Karla, Scott, and Ken, whose fellowship and love inspired me to write it.

The definition of sin is,

Missing the mark.

Your true life is hidden with Christ in God.

—Colossians 3:3

Preface

Christianity is under siege today! Most of its detractors are people from other cultures who believe their religion and politics are the right ones. However, a percentage of the detractors are people who have tried Christianity but found that they couldn't follow all the "rules" to be a Christian and who are very put off by anyone trying to "convert" them. Nevertheless, if Christianity is so hard, then what inspired first-century Christians to lay down their lives for it?

Contents

1	Challenging Unworkable Beliefs	1
2	Understanding the Two Selves	7
3	The Body Acts by Itself	13
4	A Self-Driving Car	17
5	Where Does the "Old Man" Come From?	23
6	Free Will	33
7	The Sovereignty of God	41
8	Resting in Christ	45
9	Union with God	51
10	What Are We?	53
11	The Romans Seven Syndrome	57
12	How the Body/Mind Works	61
13	Forgiveness	67
14	God Is Not "Fixing Us Up" for Heaven	69
15	We Are Being Lived	71
16	About The Author	75

1

Challenging Unworkable Beliefs

When this writer was a preteen, my parents began going to church, and naturally, they sent me to Sunday school. However, I was never told the "secret" teachings of how to live a real Christian life. It was all about salvation. But the only teachings on how to actually live the life were not biblical but rather mostly secular morality stories and homilies that were soon forgotten.

This secret is an open secret in plain sight in the Bible. But no one ever explained it to me. Now I see that they themselves didn't know either! And

I never suspected that all my effort and trying to be good only made it worse!

Being a Christian was very difficult for me; I always felt guilty, and I soon wearied of the effort and forgot about Christianity for a while. Everything called for willpower, and I was often lacking or, most often, just forgot. Nevertheless, I still felt drawn to God and often wondered about this.

In my thirties I made a real breakthrough. I discovered that there was a true self, hidden in Christ, and wrote a book about walking in the kingdom in the present day called The Present Kingdom of God.

Yet I still felt there was more to it. It wasn't until some years later that the final key was discovered. And I am sharing it in this book. It actually releases the power of God in your life when deeply understood.

Possibly this has happened to you at some point in your life: you decided to become a Christian but then found it very difficult to live the Christian life. All too often we form a mental picture in our minds of how a Christian should act and then try to be like Jesus. But it isn't real. And it doesn't work. You feel guilty.

You soon find (if you are conscientious) that it is impossible, especially for things you feel are truly "sins!" You make up your mind to conquer one particular sin, however, to your surprise, it comes back with a vengeance, worse than ever! After you go through this "exercise" a few dozen times or more, you soon become a lot less zealous. Of course, you are frustrated and feel guilty and angry each time you "relapse." You ask God for help, yet no help comes.

People are quick to tell us what we should do, but no one can tell us how. They just tell us to try harder. So there are a few things you probably were never told when you decided to become a Christian, and that has made all the difference. This book will help you to understand yourself and why you think and act as you do.

In these pages we are exploring this conundrum that has needlessly hampered Christians for two thousand years. Yet it is nothing "added on" to Christianity or removed from it. It's all right there in the Bible, but you have been blinded to this simple solution. I know I was until I prayed deeply that I could know God as He is, even though I gain nothing from it.

This is not a book of spiritual prose to inspire you. Nor is it about what you must do or how you should think. And it is not about how to get stuff out of God. It is simply a book of information about the Bible and what it is! This book does not ask us to do or think anything. Nevertheless, as this deeper understanding dawns, what you will have read will spontaneously elevate your life and actions by understanding only. No willpower is needed: "Wisdom is the principal thing; therefore, get wisdom: and with all thy getting get understanding" (Prov. 4:7).

"How can this be?" we may ask. Don't we have to know and practice what is right in order to change? The answer is no! We will find that we truly cannot do anything as the originator of our own actions, thoughts, and beliefs. You, as yourself, "me," cannot do anything—nada, zilch, zip. You, as "you," have never actually done anything in your life! "Me" is just a hazy mental image and a feeling. This is not just more "religion" but simply liberating truth about our body and mind! "For in him we live, and move, and have our being" (Acts 17:28). Take this verse literally.

2

Understanding the Two Selves

There are two selves spoken of in the New Testament: a true self and the old man (also called “the old nature,” “the flesh,” etc.). Most people think that the old man is just the bad side of their self. Nothing could be farther from the truth. The distinctions are important and can mean the difference between a life of love and fellowship with God, and a life of struggle.

We all grow up thinking our mind and body are “me.” Years ago, there was a sage named Douglas Harding who told us that we get our understanding of who and what we are from other people. We have acquired an image of ourselves made by other people's remarks. It starts when we are very young. We begin to form ideas and a self-image about ourselves.

The problem with this self-image we build is that it is not only false, it's quite unstable, not to mention completely imaginary! It is just a vague, ever-shifting image in the mind that has no stability, so that whatever our self-image is, it is continually vulnerable to other people's opinions of us as well as our own opinion. Also, circumstances can throw this self-picture for a loop. This false self can't do anything itself, but its presence in the mind spawns all kinds of fears, needs, and baser desires. It's what makes us self-centered, but we try to act as though we aren't.

And so it goes all our life. We feel the fear and confusion of the shifting sands of "me." It makes our life miserable. If someone makes an unkind remark about us, it affects our unstable self-image, and this results in fear, self-doubt, and lack of confidence. Even if you are praised and worshipped, it would still be false. On the other hand, your true self always knows what to do, and does it.

A lot has happened since biblical times, and we can now better understand how the mind and body really work. It is much clearer what the Bible's "old man" or "old nature" is. We will find that our thoughts and actions are not really ours but a series of *chain reactions* within the mind and body. As we understand the facts in this book, it works by itself: "Faith cometh by hearing and hearing by the word of God" (Rom. 10:17)!

If it is truth to the mind, it will operate spontaneously. All our senses—seeing, hearing, touching, tasting, and smelling—are monitored by the automatic thought process (mind). Memory automatically connects with similar occurrences, so that occurrences can be related to past experience. Then details of past experiences are compared by the mind as to whether the occurrence is good or bad for the imagined "me." We are then guided by our strongest desires and fears. This is what "the knowledge of good and evil" means.

It all works together by cause and effect in a chain reaction, like the domino effect or a Rube Goldberg invention where each sequence automatically sets off the next and is even predictable if all the facts are known. This is all happening below our conscious level, all unknown and unsuspected on the surface. We are *being lived* by the desires and fears caused by an imaginary entity we believe is "me," not a real person.

Circumstances trigger a reaction (never an original action) according to what facts the thought mechanism (via memory) is reminded of.

This is actually happening to you, the reader, right now, below the conscious level at this moment, a bit like a pinball bouncing from one post to another.

If a physical reaction is required, the appropriate body parts are made ready for a response. The thoughts to do these actions and movements come to consciousness as an imminent action, and then the physical response is created and triggered. The only thing that may reach full consciousness is the intent, just before the reaction happens, within a split second. We believe this is free will, but it is not. It is all cause and effect! However, we *feel* it is us doing it. Nevertheless, the action was already decided earlier, automatically, below consciousness. It was all an *automatic* reaction to the stimulus. No entity "me" is actually doing it! Think about the times you have had to think of a reason for an action after you have done it!

3

The Body Acts by Itself

There are many parts of the body that we know operate automatically without input from any "me." For instance, the iris of the eye automatically responds to light to allow just the right amount of light into the eye. Or take the heart: it beats faster or slower as needed without any conscious input. There are many bodily functions that also seem to work by themselves. See how many automatic functions you can recognize, such as digesting the meal just eaten, and so on.

How many things were found? The short answer is *all of our body/mind functions and actions work by themselves, automatically.* And it is happening right now as you read this! Therefore, all our life is lived automatically, with no actual autonomous self deciding anything. The self, the "me" that the mind thinks is "who I am," is only an imaginary self-image. There is no free will or a self to have it. Without Christ, we are no more than an organic robot or a zombie! All our actions are automatic, habitual reactions built upon our self-image, the "old man."

Wait! Do not put this book down because it says something unbelievable, or something you don't like, or something contrary to your previous teachings! Some people may not believe this. Not until they understand it. That is all it takes. This is the great secret! We are not living our own lives. We are *being lived* by an imaginary, nonexistent self! "He that findeth his life shall lose it. And he that loseth his life for my sake shall find it" (Matt. 10:39).

Note: If you cannot understand something in this book right away, you must just hold on to it until you can see *how* it could be true. Also, repeated reading will greatly help to increase your understanding.

4

A Self-Driving Car

In fact, we can compare our physical body and mind to a *self-driving car*. A car that drives itself without a driver to guide it. A self-driving car doesn't know that it exists, is not conscious, yet drives itself. The body/mind is like that car. The sensors are like our five senses, and the computers are like our brain. The body/mind *works by itself* without anybody to will it. It is what the Bible calls "the old man" or "old nature." This author often calls it the false self or "illusory" self. It is mostly made up of desires and fears because the vulnerable self-concept, the old man, attracts them. This is why we cannot live without "sinning." This, then, is why most people grow up thinking their mind and body is who they are and struggle with it all their lives.

But we don't have to crucify this old nature. It is just the *automatic, habitual* actions caused by the body/mind belief. Nevertheless, we are not the body/mind as we have imagined. We are not the old nature. God has a better way! We are now the new man in Christ: "For if we have been planted together in the likeness of his death, we shall be also in the likeness of his resurrection" (Rom. 6:5).

And we don't have to do anything to get rid of it. All it is is a mental image we believe is "what-we-are." It will begin to dissolve when we understand what it actually is and how it all works. Like a magician's trick, when you know how it works, it is no longer believed. But some habits die hard; yet some change is immediate. Further change will be more gradual. When you are walking in the Spirit, you are walking in the Kingdom!

The problem with the imaginary self-image we build is that it is not only false, it is quite unstable, not to mention that it is completely imaginary. How we feel about ourselves can change at any moment because we think this illusion is us. Yet it is just a vague, ever-shifting mental image in memory that has no stability or permanence whatsoever. Whatever our self-image is, it is continually vulnerable to other people's opinions. Also, circumstances can throw this self-picture for a loop. And so it goes all our life.

If someone makes an unkind remark about us, it affects our precious self-concept, and the result is fear, self-doubt, and a lack of confidence, even anger. We feel the fear and confusion from the presence of this unstable mental picture. It can make our lives miserable. We may think it is just "ego," but there is no such thing. It's the results of the "old man." If only Freud had read the Bible!

We are *in Christ* and have a new nature. We are the "new man" of the Bible: "I am crucified with Christ: nevertheless, I live; yet not I, but Christ liveth in me: and the life which I now live in the flesh I live by the faith of the Son of God, who loved me, and gave himself for me" (Gal. 2:20).

The old nature isn't a real "self." It is not a self that can do anything. That "me" is imaginary. Then how does the old nature affect us? The fact is that the old nature, the old man, the imaginary "me," the assumed self, *doesn't do* anything on its own. Of course it can't. But simply the *belief* in it influences the mind and memory, and this affects our actions and thoughts. We are then supremely devoted to ourselves. We are caring for a self that doesn't exist! The joke's on us! But who or what is "us"?

Just look for a self right now! Can you locate a self anywhere in your body? Of course not, because it never did exist! It is just an idea that the mind acquired as a child because all the people you knew treated you as though you were a separate object, your body, that directs and moves your actions and speech. People did this unknowingly because it is what they were taught.

5

Where Does the "Old Man" Come From?

When we are first born, the mind does not realize that we have a body, and we have no conscious connection with our bodies. Hunger is felt, and pain, and discomfort. And if we make a noise, someone will take care of our problem. That's instinct. Yet where did that idea of "me" come from? We certainly didn't make a conscious decision to think that it exists. Where did that idea come from? It happens because hunger and discomfort are unpleasant for the body, and the nervous system automatically responds with a noise. The worse the discomfort, the louder the cry.

Since this works for food and comfort, it is reinforced and strengthened and becomes a habit. When we want attention, we make a noise. In fact, we still do that, don't we? These actions are not consciously done, but they work and soon become automatic, habitual responses. Soon the automatic response of crying rises to the conscious level and we begin to be consciously aware of what is happening. This is an example of early cause and effect operating in our bodily thoughts and reactions. Thus, we learn to fuss whenever we want or need something. This is the bare beginning of what we will later believe is our *free will*. Nevertheless, it is just a habit caused by repeated occurrences.

As we get a few days and weeks older, we sense crying happening and begin to assign it to this body and *feel* that "what-we-are" did this noise. By hearing and seeing and feeling, we also begin to feel that "what-we-are" is moving and operating our body. During this time, we are effectively living in the Kingdom of Heaven and that's wonderful as far as it goes, however, since our identification with the body as "me" is not yet very strong, we still live quite spontaneously. Nevertheless, the mind's identification with the body grows stronger with more mental connections: "Verily I say unto you, except ye be converted, and become as little children, ye shall not enter into the kingdom of heaven," and "But Jesus said, 'Suffer little children, and forbid them not, to come unto me: for of such is the kingdom of heaven'" (Matt. 18:3, 19:14).

At ages one to four or five we know *that* we are because of the sense of here and now, or "I am," but not *what* we are. Others in our life influence us to identify with the body simply because they believe it. It is quite easy to adopt the identification with the body/mind because everyone treats us and communicates with us as if we are our body/mind. So, naturally, we accept that as true.

Thus, as this belief solidifies, we learn to conceptualize and objectify ourselves and begin to relate to the environment in terms of whether something is *good* or *bad* for the body/mind, our assumed self. So, sadly, our beginnings in the Kingdom fade away as we begin to identify with our body as what we are. After all, we have a name and it means "me." And we join the rest of humanity as a fallen being.

This is what Adam and Eve, using their new ability of conceptual thought, did to cause their "fall" from walking with and living spontaneously with the Holy Spirit. We may call this conceptual ability the "split-mind": "Who told you that you were naked?" (Gen. 3:11).

God knew they had eaten from the tree and identified with their bodies as their self. But how? You see, before they ate from the tree of the knowledge of *good and evil,*__they didn't conceptualize as we do now. They just rested in the Spirit and spontaneously did what was appropriate at the moment. Maybe it was just the act of disobeying God or eating whatever the "fruit" was that enabled them to think by conceptualizing. They then conceptualized their bodies as what they were, as an object, their "self." And then good and evil (bad) now had *come into the world* according to *how the world affected their body/mind!* The story of Adam and Eve gives us clues and symbols to show us what happened. It explains "the Fall" as man acquiring the ability to conceptualize and thus think. Few people in the world know and understand this fact. Now you do too!

The pride of life, the lust of the flesh, the lust of the eyes is of this world. (1 John 2:16)

This I say then, walk in the Spirit, and ye shall not fulfil the lust of the flesh. But if ye be led of the Spirit, ye are not under the law. (Gal. 5:18)

It is true that *everything* we do, if not done in the Spirit, is sin:

But the fruit of the Spirit is love, joy, peace, longsuffering, gentleness, goodness, faith, Meekness, temperance: against such there is no law. And they that are Christ's have crucified the flesh with the affections and lusts.

If we live in the Spirit, let us also walk in the Spirit. (Gal. 5:22-25)

These are not parceled out as separate gifts to different people. It is all available in the Spirit:

For we walk by faith, not by sight. (2 Cor. 5:7)

For ye were sometimes darkness, but now are ye light in the Lord: walk as children of light: 'For the fruit of the Spirit is in all goodness and righteousness and truth;' (Eph. 5:8–9)

You may be walking with the Spirit and not even realize it because it doesn't lead you in an obvious way, with a thought such as "Help that poor beggar standing at the curb." No! That's just the imagination and conscience. And that hasn't worked before, has it? We couldn't even follow the original Ten Commandments. Instead of following some imaginary spiritual prompt or mental voice, when we are in the Spirit, *we just do it!* Without deliberation!

In fact, the Ten Commandments were given *to show us that we couldn't follow them.* This is the way out of that dilemma: *when we are walking with the Spirit, we don't need prompting.* We don't need any prompting when we are resting in Christ. In fact, we don't even need to think. We will, with no deliberation, follow an indefinable urge and it just happens spontaneously! We just have an urge to do it.

In fact, isn't it when we are trying hard to do good that we often don't? We do the opposite! And aren't we trying to avoid those struggles we have with our lives going the wrong way? Sin isn't just doing "bad" things. It is doing anything that is not in the Spirit:

For we know that the law is spiritual, but I am of the flesh, sold under sin. For I do not understand my own actions. For I do not do what I want, but I do the very thing I hate. Now if I do what I do not want, I agree with the law, that it is good. So now it is not me that is, in my flesh. For I have the desire to do what is right, but not the ability to carry it out. For I do not do the good I want, but the evil I do not want is what I keep on doing. Now if I do what I do not want, it is no longer I who do it, but sin that dwells within me [the old man]. (Rom. 7:14-20)

The real blessing is we no longer have to *try* to not sin. It just happens by itself when we rest in this "New Self," Christ. However, we can't think that our life will now be sinless and we will be perfect. Sorry! That won't happen either. The mind would give the credit to the "me."

Yet, it isn't "me," it's the Spirit. We are just...being. And that's all one needs to "do"!

Often, when we are resting in Christ, we don't even realize that we are walking with the Spirit until later, if at all: "Therefore, there is now no condemnation to those who are in Christ, who walk not after the flesh, but after the spirit" (Rom. 8:1)

6

Free Will

You have not chosen me; I have chosen you.

—John 15:16

So where does free will come into this? If we watch our thoughts carefully as they happen, we will see that thoughts just happen automatically, continually. If we decide to think about something else—that' also an automatic thought. Thoughts and memories just appear automatically, triggered by association with memory and deeper thoughts below consciousness. No one is actually deciding to think. It just happens.

Nowhere in the Bible does it say that God gave us free will. We just assumed it at the Fall and *that's the problem.* We can't please God using our own "free will." (Yet the true self always knows what to do.) See Romans Chapter 7.

Now we can understand that what we thought was who we really were is just an imaginary mental picture in the mind that changes and morphs with every event. It affects our emotions with every event, whether it is good or bad for the imaginary self. This self-image isn't who we are. It's not anybody. And, therefore, it couldn't have a will, let alone a free will. So then, why does it *feel* like we are in control of this body/mind?

We are not the mind. The mind is not us thinking. Even though the mind is not us or ours, *it thinks it is*! The mind sometimes pictures itself as a thing we *are* or, at other times, a thing we *have*. But it's not a thing, it is merely a thought process that operates *automatically by association with the strongest beliefs, desires, and fears. It is not operated by any "me."*

Thoughts happen automatically and continuously. If we think we control our thoughts, just try to stop thinking. We will just think about stopping thoughts. Thoughts just happen automatically or "by themselves" through association. So there isn't any "me" deciding to think. The deciding thought happens automatically (influenced by the self-image in memory and mind).

Therefore, free will is impossible. There is no self, "me," here to do it. There is no "decision" to think. There is just another thought. If we had to decide to think something, we would first have to decide to decide. But before that we would have to decide to decide to decide, and so on forever, and it would never happen.

There is no self called "me." This is one of the most difficult things to understand, but persevere. And beautiful, spiritual, prose—no matter how true—will not help us live any better. "Seeming acts of volition merely arise spontaneously (whether caused, uncaused, or probabilistically inclined, it makes no difference) and cannot be traced to a point of origin in our conscious minds. A moment or two of serious self-scrutiny, and you might observe that you no more decide the next thought you think than the next thought I write." (Sam Harris, Will Power, 2012) The following verses prove there is no free will at all:

A man's heart deviseth his way; but Jahweh directeth his steps. (Prov 16:9)

The king's heart is in the hand of Jahweh as the watercourses: He turneth it whithersoever he will. (Prov. 21:1) For it is God who worketh in you both to will and to work, for his good pleasure. (Philippians 2:13)

He turned their heart to hate his people, to deal subtly with his servants. (Psalms 105:25)
No man can come to me, except the father that sent me draw him: and I will raise him up in the last day. (John 6:44)
And a certain woman named Lydia, a seller of purple, of the city of Thyatira, one that worshipped God, heard us: whose heart the Lord opened to give heed unto the things which were spoken by Paul. (Acts 16:14)

And all the inhabitants of the earth are reputed as nothing; and he doeth according to his will in the army of heaven, and among the inhabitants of the earth: and none can stay his hand, or say unto him "What doest thou?" (Dan. 4:35)
In whom also we were made a heritage, having been foreordained according to the purpose of him who worketh all things after the counsel of his will. (Eph. 1:11)

So, then it is not of him that willeth, nor of him that runneth, but of God that hath mercy. (Rom. 9:16)

So, then he hath mercy on whom he will, and whom he will he hardeneth. (Rom. 9:18)

Or hath not the potter a right over the clay, from the same lump to make one part a vessel unto honor, and another unto dishonor? (Rom. 9:21)

O Jahweh, I know that the way of man is not in himself; it is not in man that walketh to direct his steps. (Jer. 10:23) I will heal their backsliding, I will love them freely, for mine anger is turned away from him. (Hos. 14:4)

For the creation was subjected to vanity, not of its own will, but by reason of him who subjected it, in hope. (Rom. 8:20)

For as through the one man's disobedience the many were made sinners, even so through the obedience of the one shall the many be made righteous. (Rom. 5:19)

For God hath shut up all unto disobedience, that he might have mercy upon all. (Rom. 11:32)

7

The Sovereignty of God

Since we have discovered that our free will is an illusion, then we find a greater role for sovereignty. Sovereignty means that everything that happens was determined at the creation, at the foundation of the world. God is in total control of every aspect of our lives, no matter how minute.

Everything happens as it *must*. Your life is predestined like a movie film that's already in the can. You are the *watching* of it!

I am.

Have you ever noticed your sense of being? The sense that you are here, now, and that you exist. (Without a label, "me")

This is the sense of "*I am*." We all have this sense of "*I am*." And it is the same sense of being that God has. He is sharing his own sense of "*I am*" with each of us.

Notice your sense of "*I am*," now…

That's what we are! Within this "*I am*," is ourselves and the universe.

God didn't create the universe then set himself apart from it. Phenomenally it *is* him! The entire universe, including ourselves is God exclaiming "*I am*"!

Everything in the universe, from the largest black hole to one's own life and thoughts is God manifesting himself.

All we observe is triggered by cause and effect. Therefore, at the foundation of the world, we were created and predestined to think and do exactly what we think and do.

Do not mourn your lost free will. You never had it. It was an illusion. Instead, God is manifesting the universe, and us, according to His sovereign good will.

"The Lord will fight for you and you will hold your peace and remain at rest." Exodus 14:14.

Can we see now how much easier it is to forgive others if we know, by experience, they were predestined to do what they did? Not only that, we can now accept forgiveness for ourselves for the same reason.

Now, this isn't an excuse to sit around and do nothing. In fact, we can try it, if we want. We will find that we just can't do it for very long. We will become bored quite soon and *have* to do something. Nor is this an excuse to do evil. Much more could be said about this subject, but you have probably already heard it all before. Just appreciate God's grace for what it has cost Him. Some may see this as "cheap grace," nevertheless, it isn't if you are trusting and resting in God.

8

Resting in Christ

Instead, it is an invitation to *rest* in Christ:

Come unto me, all ye that labor and are heavy laden, and I will give you rest. Take my yoke upon you and learn of me; for I am meek and lowly in heart: and ye shall find rest unto your souls. For my yoke is easy, and my burden is light. (Matt. 11:28–30)

Before I understood the things in this book, I couldn't see how this could be true. I had mostly known guilt as a Christian. Whenever we think of "resting in Christ," it means to trust in, rely upon, and adhere to Christ. This allows the "new man," the true self. This is how we can completely surrender ourselves to God. Actually, we have *no other option*! And because of predestination, we can also more easily accept God's forgiveness for ourselves:

And he said, "My presence shall go with thee, and I will give thee rest." (Exod. 33:14)

That ye put off concerning the former conversation the old man, which is corrupt according to the deceitful lusts; And be renewed in the spirit of your mind: And that ye put on the new man, which after God is created in righteousness and true holiness. (Eph. 4:2-24)

And God blessed the seventh day and sanctified it: because that in it he had rested from all his work which God created and made. (Gen. 2:3)

Truly my soul waiteth upon God: from him cometh my salvation. He only is my rock and my salvation; he is my defense. (Ps. 62:1–2)

Return unto thy rest, O my soul; for the Lord hath dealt bountifully with thee. (Ps. 116:7)

We may think that we are pleasing God by doing things for Him: things such as holding prayer meetings, or teaching Sunday School, or feeding homeless people. We can find lots of things where we feel we are doing "God's work." Yet it counts as sin if not in the Spirit: "So then, they that are in the flesh [the old man] cannot please God" (Rom. 8:8).

To truly rest in Christ, we need to understand that it is not just laying down and sleeping. Nor does it mean to do other things. It's a mental rest. Now we can relax. God's rest is special! We have been erroneously taught that we must first do certain things before God can bless us. It's based on "Do this and you shall have that," such as "promise, problem, provision." However, that's backward; God works the other way around. God says, "You have; therefore, you can do." In this case it means "You have God's Spirit; therefore, you can do His will." In truth, the secret of rest is in *neither doing nor not doing!* This kind of rest is resting in Christ:

Know ye not that your body is the temple of the Holy Spirit, which is in you, which ye have of God, and ye are not your own? For ye are bought with a price: therefore, glorify God in your body, and in your spirit, which are God's. (1 Cor. 5: 19-20)

Trust in the Lord with all your heart, and do not lean on your own understanding." (Prov. 3:5)

So God is saying neither do nor not do in your own understanding.

Resting in Christ is neither doing nor not doing anything from our own mind and body. They are disengaged! Neither trying nor refraining. The term "let" means the best way to rest. (For example: let your life be lived by your true self.) Expect Christ to use the situation according to his own good will. Simply relax, wait, and trust in, rely on, and adhere to Christ! This is a relaxed, quiet mind and body:

Abide in me, and I in you. As the branch cannot bear fruit of itself, except it abide in the vine; no more can ye, except ye abide in me. I am the vine, ye are the branches: He that abideth in me, and I in him, the same bringeth forth much fruit: for without me ye can do nothing. (John 15: 4, 5)

9

Union with God

There is actually no false self to have union with God. Obviously, the imaginary me can never have union with God. *Your true life is hidden with Christ in God.* You *already* are one with God in Christ! Once we deeply understand the things in this book, the Bible will open to us, and our understanding will also be opened.

10

What Are We?

So far, we have found out what we are not, i.e. the old man, but that raises the question, what are we? Seeing what we are is like an eye trying to see itself. Yet, even then, an eye is an object, and what we are could not be an object. In fact, anything we can observe or see couldn't be us or ours because we are Spirit: "But you are not in the flesh, but in the Spirit, if the spirit of God dwell in you" (Rom. 8:9).

However, we can sense "what-we-are." It is the bare sense of "I am." Notice it now. What does it mean? Just say "I am" and notice.

This sense of "I am" is God's own sense of "I am" He shares with us: "God breathed the Spirit into Adam" (Gen. 2:7).

And all we can say about ourselves is that we are here, now. We need to realize that there is nothing else we could be but the bare sense of "I am." Our old man is considered dead and Christ is our life. Therefore, we are nothing tangible at all and never have been.

This body is a convenient arrangement to interact with the world as an interface. We know our world with five senses: seeing, hearing, tasting, touching, and smelling. And there could be even more senses we haven't understood yet. Our sense of "I am" is also called "Pure Awareness." Pure Awareness is a label for the sense of "I am." Within this Pure Awareness is the entire universe! This is our phenomenal being. We are nothing that appears because we are the light in which our world appears: "The eye with which I see God is the same with which God sees me" Meister Eckhart "I am that I am" (Exod. 3:14).

11

The Romans Seven Syndrome

For we know that the law is spiritual, but I am of the flesh, sold under sin. For I do not understand my own actions. For I do not do what I want, but I do the very thing I hate. Now if I do what I do not want, I agree with the law, that it is good. So now it is no longer I who do it, but sin that dwells within me. For I know that nothing good dwells in me, that is, in my flesh. (The old man) For I have the desire to do what is right, but not the ability to carry it out. For I do not do the good I want, but the evil I do not want is what I keep on doing.

Now if I do what I do not want, it is no longer I who do it, but sin that dwells within me.

—Romans 7:14–19

"If I am dead in Christ, then why do I keep sinning?" Many Christians are hypocrites because they erroneously believe that they have a good side and a bad side, and that as a Christian, they must suppress the bad side and show the good side. That is what causes *all* our problems.

This is *why* we end up doing the wrong things. Sinning is any action not done in the Spirit. Remember now that the old nature is just an automatically acting mind and body. It is just an organic automaton built in the mind on the belief that it is "me." This makes us self-centered, and *all* actions originating from beliefs in the false self are automatically oriented on the imaginary self-image. That imaginary self is entirely dedicated to protecting, enhancing, and satisfying the needs and desires of the false self, "me." Yet that self will never be in heaven because the imaginary self (old man) automatically reacts to fulfill the lusts spawned by the desires within the old man and to "protect" this imaginary self from anything bad.

This is why, the harder we *try* to be a "good" person, the more we identify with this *imaginary self*. And what happens then? We do the selfish action because we have *activated* the imaginary self which automatically sins. Thus, we sin and don't realize why because we are trying to be a good person. But what happens when we try to be a good person? What happens when we try to use what we think is our volition? The old nature is triggered because we activated the old nature belief by *trying*.

Trying to use volition (willpower) of the illusory self (the old man) affirms it, thereby activating the needs and desires it embodies, giving them power. The result is "that I do not." See Romans 7:15-17. Volition is an illusion! Trying to use the volition of the imaginary, conceptual self affirms the conceptual self and only activates the desires and fears linked to it, giving them power.

The results are "For that which I do I allow not: for what I would, that do I not; but what I hate, that do I" (Rom. 7:15). Recognize that there is no "me" doing any of it. It's all just happening automatically:

- Actually, nothing I do is me or mine or "my" doing. I can now relax!
- By relying on volition or will, we awaken the false self-belief and its needs.
- Anything not done in the Spirit is sin!

"For the law of the Spirit of life in Christ Jesus, has made me free from the law of sin and death" (Rom,) 8:2. Do realize that this is freedom!

12

How the Body/Mind Works

The "mind" is not a *thing*, it is an automatic thought-processor, a processor that automatically evaluates every thought and experience against one's deepest desires and fears in memory. Our thoughts and actions are caused by neural activity below the conscious level; however, this makes the concept of free will untenable.

If we carefully observe ourselves, we will see a chain reaction of thoughts and the resulting actions. The laws of cause and effect are clearly in action. Now, many actions are triggered by other thoughts and memories, but they are below the conscious level, and we don't realize that this is happening. The old man can only cause a reaction and cannot act originally. This then, means that the laws of cause and effect are operating.

That points us directly to predestination:

And we know that all things work together for good to them that love God, to them who are the called according to his purpose. For whom he did foreknow, he also did predestinate to be conformed to the image of his Son, that he might be the firstborn among many brethren.

Moreover, whom he did predestinate, them he also called: and whom he called, them he also justified: and whom he justified, them he also glorified. (Rom. 8:29–31)

You have not chosen me, but I have chosen you. (John 15:16)

You may find some disagreement on this point from others who are not aware of this, even other

Christians who are not aware of this. Possibly one's own sensibilities are rebelling about this. And the answer is both yes and no. For one's false self-image is predestined, not your true life in Christ. However, in God's time it all has already happened.

This may feel like free will because when we identify with the body/mind and then do something through it, it *seems* like it was "me," but as we have seen, that is not "what-we-are" but the old nature is predestined and foreordained to do exactly as it has done.

Our life is like a movie already produced and "in the can," and we just watch it. Like the kiddie cars at the zoo, you have a steering wheel, but it's the little slot down the middle of the track that actually guides the cars. Yet the children think they are driving. The steering wheel is like our willpower. The slot is like predestination. Yet, if you let go of the wheel, you will drive perfectly!

How many times has a long-sought answer to a question or problem just "come to us" all of a sudden? This is an excellent example of the mind working below the conscious level automatically by cause and effect and association.

If the whole universe happens by cause and effect, then that has to be true for the mind also. And, with some serious self-observation (of thoughts and actions), one will surely be convinced that all of our actions are determined! Volition is an illusion! *Trying* to use the volition of the imaginary self only activates the desires and fears linked to the imaginary self, giving them power. The result is "What I would, that I do not; but what I hate, that I do" (Rom. 7:15):

- See that there is no "me" doing any of it. It's all just happening.
- Actually, nothing "I" do is me or mine or "my" doing. I can now relax and live joyfully!

- By relying on volition, our supposed will, we awaken the false self-belief and its baser needs.
- Anything not done in the Spirit is sin!

"I live by the faith of the Son of God, who loved me and gave himself for me" (Gal. 2:20).

God even gives us the faith we need!

13

Forgiveness

Jesus is the "lamb slain from the foundation of the world."

—Revelation 13:80

Jesus' death on the cross took the blame for all our sins done in the false, imaginary self, in the old man. Walking in the Spirit does not arouse the desires and fears of this false "me." And it allows God to manifest His will through our body. Some people seem to act as though, while we are forgiven, when we become a Christian we must confess and get forgiven all over again every time we sin. It's okay to do that if it helps you to feel better. But what things are sins? Actually, a sin is any action not performed in the Spirit. Otherwise, we are reacting from the needs and fears of the old man.

Nevertheless, we are continually cleansed because of "the lamb slain from the foundation of the world" (Rev. 13:80). So we don't have to get forgiveness again every time we sin. And that's important so we can rest and not worry about sinning. Therefore, we are free to rest in Christ and walk with the Spirit.

In God is all of space-time, so we can rely on salvation covering all time: forward and backward. In this sense, we have always been "saved," yet we only become Christians in our lifetime. This takes the pressure off trying to not sin. At the same time, the old nature is *not* activated because we are not trying to use our own volition which triggers it.

14

God Is Not "Fixing Us Up" for Heaven

This is a common attitude among many, that God is making us better for heaven. Have you ever seen a "perfected" person ready for heaven? No one has. So that can't be true. "God hasn't finished with me yet!" This is usually said jokingly, but it is at the basis of thinking that difficulties are sent to us by God to teach us something. While it may help to get us through a difficult time, there is a better way. Wouldn't it be much better if we faced these difficulties while walking with the Spirit? That's the most important thing we can learn.

The self we think we are is dead in Christ.

Why then would God want to perfect the illusory self? At the same time, we have the perfect life of Christ to *live us*.

15

We Are Being Lived

Can we now see that we are not living our own lives? The imaginary "me" has no power at all. When we rely on our own "willpower," it leads to sin. We cannot be who we *think* we are. That's just the imaginary self, "me." We have no other option but to rely on the Spirit of Christ. *We are always being lived*, either by the "old man" or the Spirit of Christ. Christ will live our life for us if we just let him. Nevertheless, we must be open to allowing Christ to do as he wills, even if it doesn't fit our preconceived plans and desires. God asks nothing from us, yet is giving us the universe.

We may be dismayed by the life God has given us. Let it be an adventure! We will find that if we trust Christ, we often have outcomes that surprise us. They are usually different from our preconceived notions. Some of our worst sources of frustration are when things don't go as we want them. But remember, many times things actually work out better than in our imagination. So go ahead and follow your dreams, but sometimes we just need to wait and see. Let your life be lived by your true self! *Live joyfully!* And follow your sense of wonder.

If this book has had a positive impact on your life, you might want to start a weekly or monthly study group with other Christian friends.

Read and discuss a chapter each meeting. Some chapters you might want to take more time to discuss. Have fun and spread the joy.

About The Author

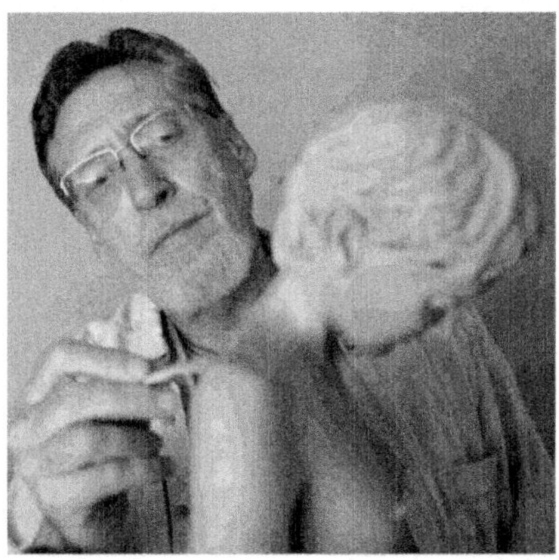

Galen Sharp has written several books about living the Christian life. He says this is his best yet.

Galen says that it was like finding the holy grail when it all came together for him and hopes the same for the readers.

Other Book by The Author

The Present Kingdom of God

Galen shows us through scripture and actual experience that oneness with God is our true, natural state. With this momentous discovery, readers will recognize for themselves that the Kingdom of God is available here and now and that "Walking in the Spirit" is the lost secret to effortless living.

Non-Dual Teaching of The Bible

This book paves the way to begin to see the teachings of the Bible in a whole new light. Galen Sharp skilfully and with great care and compassion guides the reader through the inner doorway of Awareness and into the Silence of the Heart.

What Am I? A Study in Non-Volitional Living

This book explores a variety of subjects such as science, philosophy, quantum physics and even some of the ancient masters in quest of a higher way of knowing the world and ourselves. Through eleven Reality Meditations you will be able to examine your own mental mechanisms and find out how they really work, examine who and what you really are.

Printed in Great Britain
by Amazon

37595527R00051